Guess What I Am

Written by Grace Davis
Illustrated by Jim Madsen

Can you guess what I am?

I don't have fins to help me swim, . . .

. . . so I am not a fish who lives in the sea.

I don't have feathers to help me fly, . . .

. . . so I can't be a bird in the sky.

I don't have scales that cover me, . . .

. . . so I am not a reptile like a crocodile.

I wasn't hatched in the water, . . .

. . . so I can't be a frog that lives in a pond.

I have hair, and I breathe air, and I walk on two legs.

I'm a person, just like you!